F Words

A Daily Check-In On Your Vision

This Journal Belongs To:

_____

My Focus Word For the Year is:

_____

Journal #   _____

Date Range:

_____ to _____

This edition published by:
eLegal Publishing
An Imprint of eLegal Cafe, LLC
1527 W. State Highway 114, Ste. 500-189
Grapevine, TX 76051

connectwithme@nadiagilkes.com

Follow me on social media

@officialnadiagilkes

@nadia.gilkes

Book Cover & Interior Design by: Van-Garde Imagery, Inc.

Edited by: Dianne Hunter

ISBN:
978-1-7332504-0-5
978-1-7332504-1-2
978-1-7332504-2-9

F Words

A Daily Check-In On Your Vision

Why This Journal?

THE YEAR 2020 THREW MANY of us for a loop. I felt blessed to make it to 2021. When a new year dawned, I felt a responsibility to live life to the fullest. Not just for myself, but for those who didn't make it. More than anything, I felt it was time to do things differently.

I started the new year by creating a vision board, something I'd heard a great deal about but had never actually tried. I hung it where I could see it every day. It helped to have a visual of where I am headed, but it wasn't enough. That's when I decided to get more intentional with my journaling.

In addition to reviewing the vision board regularly, I started to write down what actions I took each day that fed into the vision I outlined for myself. I came up with my group of F Words:

> Faith - Family - Fitness - Full Steam Ahead *(work/large projects)* - Feed My Soul *(creative outlet)* - Financial - Frolics *(fun)*.

Each day I aim to do something that fills each of these buckets. The end goal - a balanced life.

This worked wonders to help me stay focused and hold myself accountable. Over time it occurred to me that others may benefit from this same system. As a result, I've created this 90-day journal for you.

I hope it serves you as well it serves me.

Creating A Vision Board

To BEGIN, IT MAY HELP if you create a physical or electronic vision board. Vision boards are a collage of images that display your goals and dreams. The idea is to get those dreams out of your head and into a format that you can actually see. When you hang your vision board prominently and review it every day, your mind works to bring your vision to reality.

Vision boards can be as simple or elaborate as you like. The basics for a physical one include posterboard, magazines, a glue stick, and scissors. For an electronic one, you can use a Word document, Canva, or a vision board app to upload images into and arrange your collage. YouTube and Pinterest offer great ideas to get your creative juices flowing.

Before you begin to create your board, think about the long-term goals that you aim to achieve within the next year. You may find that many of your goals fit snugly into the buckets outlined on the previous page.

As you identify your goals, also think about your WHY. Why are these goals important to you? It is your WHY that will serve as your motivation in tough times and help drive you to success.

Once you've identified your goals and your WHY - write them out on the next couple of pages. Then, begin creating your board by simply cutting out images and phrases from the magazines that resonate with you and align with your goals. Arrange these images on the posterboard in a way that appeals to you and glue them down. When dry, hang your board in an area where you will see it every day.

My Goals ... My Why

Faith: _____

My Why: _____

Family: _____

My Why: _____

Fitness: _____

My Why: _____

Full Steam Ahead: _____

My Why: _____

Feed My Soul: _____

My Why: _____

Financial: _____

_____

My Why: _____

Frolics: _____

_____

My Why: _____

How To Use This Journal

IF THE IDEA OF JOURNALING seems daunting, don't fret. This one is meant to be EASY. Now that your vision and goals are identified and written out, it is time to put action behind them. When you wake up each day, look at your vision board and list 3 small actions you will accomplish today that will feed into the vision you've outlined for yourself. There are checkboxes next to each item to mark your successes as they come.

In the space next to each F word, jot down a sentence or two of how you filled that bucket each day.

Before bed, reflect and jot down three things you are grateful for. At the end of each week there is space for notes to keep track of progress or anything else you'd like to document. That's it. It's that easy!

Now you just have to get started. YOU GOT THIS!

Notes

🦋 Good Morning

Three things you will accomplish today:

❏ _____

❏ _____

❏ _____

As you move through your day, pour into yourself. Then, make note of it:

FAITH

_____

_____

_____

FAMILY

_____

_____

_____

FITNESS

_____

_____

_____

Love Yourself

Date: _____

FULL STEAM AHEAD

_____

_____

_____

FEED MY SOUL

_____

_____

_____

FINANCIAL

_____

_____

_____

FROLICS

_____

_____

_____

End your day on a good note. List three things you are grateful for:

1. _____

2. _____

3. _____

You Are Worthy

Upsie Daisie

Three things you will accomplish today:

❏ _____

❏ _____

❏ _____

As you move through your day, pour into yourself. Then, make note of it:

FAITH

_____

_____

_____

FAMILY

_____

_____

_____

FITNESS

_____

_____

_____

Forgive Yourself

Date: _____

FULL STEAM AHEAD

_____

_____

_____

FEED MY SOUL

_____

_____

_____

FINANCIAL

_____

_____

_____

FROLICS

_____

_____

_____

End your day on a good note. List three things you are grateful for:

1. _____

2. _____

3. _____

Healing Is Powerful

Rise & Grind

Three things you will accomplish today:

❑ _____

❑ _____

❑ _____

As you move through your day, pour into yourself. Then, make note of it:

FAITH

_____

_____

_____

FAMILY

_____

_____

_____

FITNESS

_____

_____

_____

Choose Yourself

Date: _____

FULL STEAM AHEAD

_____

_____

_____

FEED MY SOUL

_____

_____

_____

FINANCIAL

_____

_____

_____

FROLICS

_____

_____

_____

End your day on a good note. List three things you are grateful for:

1. _____

2. _____

3. _____

Always

Time To Conquer The Day

Three things you will accomplish today:

❏ _____

❏ _____

❏ _____

As you move through your day, pour into yourself. Then, make note of it:

FAITH

_____

_____

_____

FAMILY

_____

_____

_____

FITNESS

_____

_____

_____

Trust Yourself

Date: _____

FULL STEAM AHEAD

_____

_____

_____

FEED MY SOUL

_____

_____

_____

FINANCIAL

_____

_____

_____

FROLICS

_____

_____

_____

End your day on a good note. List three things you are grateful for:

1. _____

2. _____

3. _____

You Are Incredible

Out Of Bed, Sleepie Head

Three things you will accomplish today:

- ❑ _____
- ❑ _____
- ❑ _____

As you move through your day, pour into yourself. Then, make note of it:

FAITH

_____

_____

_____

FAMILY

_____

_____

_____

FITNESS

_____

_____

_____

Respect Yourself

Date: _____

FULL STEAM AHEAD

_____

_____

_____

FEED MY SOUL

_____

_____

_____

FINANCIAL

_____

_____

_____

FROLICS

_____

_____

_____

End your day on a good note. List three things you are grateful for:

1. _____

2. _____

3. _____

Teach Others How To Treat You

Early To Rise

Three things you will accomplish today:

❏ _____

❏ _____

❏ _____

As you move through your day, pour into yourself. Then, make note of it:

FAITH

_____

_____

_____

FAMILY

_____

_____

_____

FITNESS

_____

_____

_____

Speak Kindly To Yourself

Date: _____

FULL STEAM AHEAD

_____

_____

_____

FEED MY SOUL

_____

_____

_____

FINANCIAL

_____

_____

_____

FROLICS

_____

_____

_____

End your day on a good note. List three things you are grateful for:

1. _____

2. _____

3. _____

You Are Listening

The Day Is Unfolding

Three things you will accomplish today:

- ❏ _____
- ❏ _____
- ❏ _____

As you move through your day, pour into yourself. Then, make note of it:

FAITH

_____

_____

_____

FAMILY

_____

_____

_____

FITNESS

_____

_____

_____

Take Care Of Yourself

Date: _____

FULL STEAM AHEAD

_____

_____

_____

FEED MY SOUL

_____

_____

_____

FINANCIAL

_____

_____

_____

FROLICS

_____

_____

_____

End your day on a good note. List three things you are grateful for:

1. _____

2. _____

3. _____

Self-Care Is NOT Selfish

Notes

The Day Is Yours

Three things you will accomplish today:

❏ _____

❏ _____

❏ _____

As you move through your day, pour into yourself. Then, make note of it:

FAITH

_____

_____

_____

FAMILY

_____

_____

_____

FITNESS

_____

_____

_____

You Are Enough

Date: _____

FULL STEAM AHEAD

_____

_____

_____

FEED MY SOUL

_____

_____

_____

FINANCIAL

_____

_____

_____

FROLICS

_____

_____

_____

End your day on a good note. List three things you are grateful for:

1. _____

2. _____

3. _____

Always Have Been ... Always Will Be

Welcome To A New Day

Three things you will accomplish today:

☐ _____

☐ _____

☐ _____

As you move through your day, pour into yourself. Then, make note of it:

FAITH

_____

_____

_____

FAMILY

_____

_____

_____

FITNESS

_____

_____

_____

Be Authentic

Date: _____

FULL STEAM AHEAD

_____

_____

_____

FEED MY SOUL

_____

_____

_____

FINANCIAL

_____

_____

_____

FROLICS

_____

_____

_____

End your day on a good note. List three things you are grateful for:

1. _____

2. _____

3. _____

Walk In Your Greatness

Hello There

Three things you will accomplish today:

❏ _____

❏ _____

❏ _____

As you move through your day, pour into yourself. Then, make note of it:

FAITH

_____

_____

_____

FAMILY

_____

_____

_____

FITNESS

_____

_____

_____

Speak Your Truth

Date: _____

FULL STEAM AHEAD

_____

_____

_____

FEED MY SOUL

_____

_____

_____

FINANCIAL

_____

_____

_____

FROLICS

_____

_____

_____

End your day on a good note. List three things you are grateful for:

1. _____

2. _____

3. _____

You Are An Inspiration

Let's Do This

Three things you will accomplish today:

- ❏ _____
- ❏ _____
- ❏ _____

As you move through your day, pour into yourself. Then, make note of it:

FAITH

_____

_____

_____

FAMILY

_____

_____

_____

FITNESS

_____

_____

_____

Demand The Best

Date: _____

FULL STEAM AHEAD

_____

_____

_____

FEED MY SOUL

_____

_____

_____

FINANCIAL

_____

_____

_____

FROLICS

_____

_____

_____

End your day on a good note. List three things you are grateful for:

1. _____

2. _____

3. _____

You Deserve It

Early Bird Catches The Worm

Three things you will accomplish today:

❑ _____

❑ _____

❑ _____

As you move through your day, pour into yourself. Then, make note of it:

FAITH

_____

_____

_____

FAMILY

_____

_____

_____

FITNESS

_____

_____

_____

Know Your Worth

Date: _____

FULL STEAM AHEAD

_____

_____

_____

FEED MY SOUL

_____

_____

_____

FINANCIAL

_____

_____

_____

FROLICS

_____

_____

_____

End your day on a good note. List three things you are grateful for:

1. _____

2. _____

3. _____

... and Charge Full Price

Good Morning, Sunshine

Three things you will accomplish today:

☐ _____

☐ _____

☐ _____

As you move through your day, pour into yourself. Then, make note of it:

FAITH

_____

_____

_____

FAMILY

_____

_____

_____

FITNESS

_____

_____

_____

Believe In Yourself

Date: _____

FULL STEAM AHEAD

_____

_____

_____

FEED MY SOUL

_____

_____

_____

FINANCIAL

_____

_____

_____

FROLICS

_____

_____

_____

End your day on a good note. List three things you are grateful for:

1. _____

2. _____

3. _____

You Are Powerful

Make It A Great Day

Three things you will accomplish today:

❑ _____

❑ _____

❑ _____

As you move through your day, pour into yourself. Then, make note of it:

FAITH

_____

_____

_____

FAMILY

_____

_____

_____

FITNESS

_____

_____

_____

Today Is A Gift

Date: _____

FULL STEAM AHEAD

_____

_____

_____

FEED MY SOUL

_____

_____

_____

FINANCIAL

_____

_____

_____

FROLICS

_____

_____

_____

End your day on a good note. List three things you are grateful for:

1. _____

2. _____

3. _____

Choose Happy

Notes

Good Morning

Three things you will accomplish today:

❏ _____

❏ _____

❏ _____

As you move through your day, pour into yourself. Then, make note of it:

FAITH

_____

_____

_____

FAMILY

_____

_____

_____

FITNESS

_____

_____

_____

Love Without Conditions

Date: _____

FULL STEAM AHEAD

_____

_____

_____

FEED MY SOUL

_____

_____

_____

FINANCIAL

_____

_____

_____

FROLICS

_____

_____

_____

End your day on a good note. List three things you are grateful for:

1. _____

2. _____

3. _____

Trust Your Heart

Three things you will accomplish today:

❏ _____

❏ _____

❏ _____

As you move through your day, pour into yourself. Then, make note of it:

FAITH

_____

_____

_____

FAMILY

_____

_____

_____

FITNESS

_____

_____

_____

Give Without Expectations

Date: _____

FULL STEAM AHEAD

_____

_____

_____

FEED MY SOUL

_____

_____

_____

FINANCIAL

_____

_____

_____

FROLICS

_____

_____

_____

End your day on a good note. List three things you are grateful for:

1. _____

2. _____

3. _____

You May Change Someone's Life

Rise & Grind

Three things you will accomplish today:

- ❑ _____
- ❑ _____
- ❑ _____

As you move through your day, pour into yourself. Then, make note of it:

FAITH

_____

_____

_____

FAMILY

_____

_____

_____

FITNESS

_____

_____

_____

Live With Intention

Date: _____

FULL STEAM AHEAD

_____

_____

_____

FEED MY SOUL

_____

_____

_____

FINANCIAL

_____

_____

_____

FROLICS

_____

_____

_____

End your day on a good note. List three things you are grateful for:

1. _____

2. _____

3. _____

Your Purpose Will Reveal Itself In Time

Time To Conquer The Day

Three things you will accomplish today:

❏ _____

❏ _____

❏ _____

As you move through your day, pour into yourself. Then, make note of it:

FAITH

_____

_____

_____

FAMILY

_____

_____

_____

FITNESS

_____

_____

_____

Be Bold

Date: _____

FULL STEAM AHEAD

_____

_____

_____

FEED MY SOUL

_____

_____

_____

FINANCIAL

_____

_____

_____

FROLICS

_____

_____

_____

End your day on a good note. List three things you are grateful for:

1. _____

2. _____

3. _____

Don't Dim Your Light For Anyone

Out Of Bed, Sleepie Head

Three things you will accomplish today:

❑ _____

❑ _____

❑ _____

As you move through your day, pour into yourself. Then, make note of it:

FAITH

_____

_____

_____

FAMILY

_____

_____

_____

FITNESS

_____

_____

_____

Be Fearless

FULL STEAM AHEAD

_____

_____

_____

FEED MY SOUL

_____

_____

_____

FINANCIAL

_____

_____

_____

FROLICS

_____

_____

_____

End your day on a good note. List three things you are grateful for:

1. _____

2. _____

3. _____

Don't Stand In Your Own Way

Early To Rise

Three things you will accomplish today:

❑ _____

❑ _____

❑ _____

As you move through your day, pour into yourself. Then, make note of it:

FAITH

_____

_____

_____

FAMILY

_____

_____

_____

FITNESS

_____

_____

_____

Live Out Loud

Date: _____

FULL STEAM AHEAD

_____

_____

_____

FEED MY SOUL

_____

_____

_____

FINANCIAL

_____

_____

_____

FROLICS

_____

_____

_____

End your day on a good note. List three things you are grateful for:

1. _____

2. _____

3. _____

Don't Apologize For Being You

The Day Is Unfolding

Three things you will accomplish today:

- ❑ _____
- ❑ _____
- ❑ _____

As you move through your day, pour into yourself. Then, make note of it:

FAITH

_____

_____

_____

FAMILY

_____

_____

_____

FITNESS

_____

_____

_____

FULL STEAM AHEAD

_____

_____

_____

FEED MY SOUL

_____

_____

_____

FINANCIAL

_____

_____

_____

FROLICS

_____

_____

_____

End your day on a good note. List three things you are grateful for:

1. _____

2. _____

3. _____

You Don't Have To Carry It Forever

Notes

The Day Is Yours

Three things you will accomplish today:

❑ _____

❑ _____

❑ _____

As you move through your day, pour into yourself. Then, make note of it:

FAITH

_____

_____

_____

FAMILY

_____

_____

_____

FITNESS

_____

_____

_____

You Get To Decide

Date: _____

FULL STEAM AHEAD

_____

_____

_____

FEED MY SOUL

_____

_____

_____

FINANCIAL

_____

_____

_____

FROLICS

_____

_____

_____

End your day on a good note. List three things you are grateful for:

1. _____

2. _____

3. _____

Go After Your Desires

Welcome To A New Day

Three things you will accomplish today:

- ❑ _____
- ❑ _____
- ❑ _____

As you move through your day, pour into yourself. Then, make note of it:

FAITH

_____

_____

_____

FAMILY

_____

_____

_____

FITNESS

_____

_____

_____

Tap Into Your Talents

FULL STEAM AHEAD

_____

_____

_____

FEED MY SOUL

_____

_____

_____

FINANCIAL

_____

_____

_____

FROLICS

_____

_____

_____

End your day on a good note. List three things you are grateful for:

1. _____

2. _____

3. _____

Grab Every Opportunity

Hello There

Three things you will accomplish today:

❑ _____

❑ _____

❑ _____

As you move through your day, pour into yourself. Then, make note of it:

FAITH

_____

_____

_____

FAMILY

_____

_____

_____

FITNESS

_____

_____

_____

You Know What's Best For You

FULL STEAM AHEAD

_____

_____

_____

FEED MY SOUL

_____

_____

_____

FINANCIAL

_____

_____

_____

FROLICS

_____

_____

_____

End your day on a good note. List three things you are grateful for:

1. _____

2. _____

3. _____

Trust Your Own Advice

Let's Do This

Three things you will accomplish today:

❑ _____

❑ _____

❑ _____

As you move through your day, pour into yourself. Then, make note of it:

FAITH

_____

_____

_____

FAMILY

_____

_____

_____

FITNESS

_____

_____

_____

Don't Criticize Yourself

FULL STEAM AHEAD

_____

_____

_____

FEED MY SOUL

_____

_____

_____

FINANCIAL

_____

_____

_____

FROLICS

_____

_____

_____

End your day on a good note. List three things you are grateful for:

1. _____

2. _____

3. _____

Celebrate Yourself

Early Bird Catches The Worm

Three things you will accomplish today:

❏ _____

❏ _____

❏ _____

As you move through your day, pour into yourself. Then, make note of it:

FAITH

_____

_____

_____

FAMILY

_____

_____

_____

FITNESS

_____

_____

_____

Be Courageous

FULL STEAM AHEAD

_____

_____

_____

FEED MY SOUL

_____

_____

_____

FINANCIAL

_____

_____

_____

FROLICS

_____

_____

_____

End your day on a good note. List three things you are grateful for:

1. _____

2. _____

3. _____

Do It Afraid

Good Morning, Sunshine

Three things you will accomplish today:

❑ _____

❑ _____

❑ _____

As you move through your day, pour into yourself. Then, make note of it:

FAITH

_____

_____

_____

FAMILY

_____

_____

_____

FITNESS

_____

_____

_____

Pause. Rest. But Don't Quit.

Date: _____

FULL STEAM AHEAD

_____

_____

_____

FEED MY SOUL

_____

_____

_____

FINANCIAL

_____

_____

_____

FROLICS

_____

_____

_____

End your day on a good note. List three things you are grateful for:

1. _____

2. _____

3. _____

Your Breakthrough Is Within Reach

Make It A Great Day

Three things you will accomplish today:

❏ _____

❏ _____

❏ _____

As you move through your day, pour into yourself. Then, make note of it:

FAITH

_____

_____

_____

FAMILY

_____

_____

_____

FITNESS

_____

_____

_____

You Are Meant For Greatness

Date: _____

FULL STEAM AHEAD

_____

_____

_____

FEED MY SOUL

_____

_____

_____

FINANCIAL

_____

_____

_____

FROLICS

_____

_____

_____

End your day on a good note. List three things you are grateful for:

1. _____

2. _____

3. _____

Don't Sell Yourself Short

Notes

Good Morning

Three things you will accomplish today:

❏ _____

❏ _____

❏ _____

As you move through your day, pour into yourself. Then, make note of it:

FAITH

_____

_____

_____

FAMILY

_____

_____

_____

FITNESS

_____

_____

_____

How You See Things Means Everything

Date: _____

FULL STEAM AHEAD

_____

_____

_____

FEED MY SOUL

_____

_____

_____

FINANCIAL

_____

_____

_____

FROLICS

_____

_____

_____

End your day on a good note. List three things you are grateful for:

1. _____

2. _____

3. _____

What Do You See?

Upsie Daisie

Three things you will accomplish today:

❏ _____

❏ _____

❏ _____

As you move through your day, pour into yourself. Then, make note of it:

FAITH

_____

_____

_____

FAMILY

_____

_____

_____

FITNESS

_____

_____

_____

You Are Your Own Recovery

Date: _____

FULL STEAM AHEAD

_____

_____

_____

FEED MY SOUL

_____

_____

_____

FINANCIAL

_____

_____

_____

FROLICS

_____

_____

_____

End your day on a good note. List three things you are grateful for:

1. _____

2. _____

3. _____

Heal

Rise & Grind

Three things you will accomplish today:

❏ _____

❏ _____

❏ _____

As you move through your day, pour into yourself. Then, make note of it:

FAITH

_____

_____

_____

FAMILY

_____

_____

_____

FITNESS

_____

_____

_____

Never Give Up

Date: _____

FULL STEAM AHEAD

_____

_____

_____

FEED MY SOUL

_____

_____

_____

FINANCIAL

_____

_____

_____

FROLICS

_____

_____

_____

End your day on a good note. List three things you are grateful for:

1. _____

2. _____

3. _____

You Are Almost There

Time To Conquer The Day

Three things you will accomplish today:

☐ _____

☐ _____

☐ _____

As you move through your day, pour into yourself. Then, make note of it:

FAITH

_____

_____

_____

FAMILY

_____

_____

_____

FITNESS

_____

_____

_____

Imagine Better For Yourself

Date: _____

FULL STEAM AHEAD

_____

_____

_____

FEED MY SOUL

_____

_____

_____

FINANCIAL

_____

_____

_____

FROLICS

_____

_____

_____

End your day on a good note. List three things you are grateful for:

1. _____

2. _____

3. _____

Then Create It

Out Of Bed, Sleepie Head

Three things you will accomplish today:

- [ ] _____
- [ ] _____
- [ ] _____

As you move through your day, pour into yourself. Then, make note of it:

FAITH

_____

_____

_____

FAMILY

_____

_____

_____

FITNESS

_____

_____

_____

Everything Is Within Your Grasp

Date: _____

FULL STEAM AHEAD

_____

_____

_____

FEED MY SOUL

_____

_____

_____

FINANCIAL

_____

_____

_____

FROLICS

_____

_____

_____

End your day on a good note. List three things you are grateful for:

1. _____

2. _____

3. _____

Use Your Resources

Early To Rise

Three things you will accomplish today:

- ❏ _____
- ❏ _____
- ❏ _____

As you move through your day, pour into yourself. Then, make note of it:

FAITH

_____

_____

_____

FAMILY

_____

_____

_____

FITNESS

_____

_____

_____

Stop Sabotaging Yourself

Date: _____

FULL STEAM AHEAD

_____

_____

_____

FEED MY SOUL

_____

_____

_____

FINANCIAL

_____

_____

_____

FROLICS

_____

_____

_____

End your day on a good note. List three things you are grateful for:

1. _____

2. _____

3. _____

Create New Habits

The Day Is Unfolding

Three things you will accomplish today:

- ❏ _____
- ❏ _____
- ❏ _____

As you move through your day, pour into yourself. Then, make note of it:

FAITH

_____

_____

_____

FAMILY

_____

_____

_____

FITNESS

_____

_____

_____

Don't Cheat Yourself

Date: _____

FULL STEAM AHEAD

_____

_____

_____

FEED MY SOUL

_____

_____

_____

FINANCIAL

_____

_____

_____

FROLICS

_____

_____

_____

End your day on a good note. List three things you are grateful for:

1. _____

2. _____

3. _____

You Deserve 100% Of Your Effort

Notes

The Day Is Yours

Three things you will accomplish today:

- ☐ _____
- ☐ _____
- ☐ _____

As you move through your day, pour into yourself. Then, make note of it:

FAITH

_____

_____

_____

FAMILY

_____

_____

_____

FITNESS

_____

_____

_____

Comparison Kills Dreams

Date: _____

FULL STEAM AHEAD

_____

_____

_____

FEED MY SOUL

_____

_____

_____

FINANCIAL

_____

_____

_____

FROLICS

_____

_____

_____

End your day on a good note. List three things you are grateful for:

1. _____

2. _____

3. _____

Run Your Own Race

Welcome To A New Day

Three things you will accomplish today:

❏ _____

❏ _____

❏ _____

As you move through your day, pour into yourself. Then, make note of it:

FAITH

_____

_____

_____

FAMILY

_____

_____

_____

FITNESS

_____

_____

_____

Indecision Is Paralyzing

Date: _____

FULL STEAM AHEAD

_____

_____

_____

FEED MY SOUL

_____

_____

_____

FINANCIAL

_____

_____

_____

FROLICS

_____

_____

_____

End your day on a good note. List three things you are grateful for:

1. _____

2. _____

3. _____

Take Action

Hello There

Three things you will accomplish today:

- ☐ _____
- ☐ _____
- ☐ _____

As you move through your day, pour into yourself. Then, make note of it:

FAITH

_____

_____

_____

FAMILY

_____

_____

_____

FITNESS

_____

_____

_____

Find What Works and Repeat It

Date: _____

FULL STEAM AHEAD

_____

_____

_____

FEED MY SOUL

_____

_____

_____

FINANCIAL

_____

_____

_____

FROLICS

_____

_____

_____

End your day on a good note. List three things you are grateful for:

1. _____

2. _____

3. _____

Consistency Matters

Let's Do This

Three things you will accomplish today:

❏ _____

❏ _____

❏ _____

As you move through your day, pour into yourself. Then, make note of it:

FAITH

_____

_____

_____

FAMILY

_____

_____

_____

FITNESS

_____

_____

_____

Clear Clutter From Your Life

FULL STEAM AHEAD

_____

_____

_____

FEED MY SOUL

_____

_____

_____

FINANCIAL

_____

_____

_____

FROLICS

_____

_____

_____

End your day on a good note. List three things you are grateful for:

1. _____

2. _____

3. _____

Focus

Early Bird Catches The Worm

Three things you will accomplish today:

- ❑ ....
- ❑ ....
- ❑ ....

As you move through your day, pour into yourself. Then, make note of it:

FAITH

_____

_____

_____

FAMILY

_____

_____

_____

FITNESS

_____

_____

_____

Trust The Process

Date: _____

FULL STEAM AHEAD

_____

_____

_____

FEED MY SOUL

_____

_____

_____

FINANCIAL

_____

_____

_____

FROLICS

_____

_____

_____

End your day on a good note. List three things you are grateful for:

1. _____

2. _____

3. _____

It Will Work If You Do The Work

Good Morning, Sunshine

Three things you will accomplish today:

❏ _____

❏ _____

❏ _____

As you move through your day, pour into yourself. Then, make note of it:

FAITH

_____

_____

_____

FAMILY

_____

_____

_____

FITNESS

_____

_____

_____

Get A Mentor

Date: _____

FULL STEAM AHEAD

_____

_____

_____

FEED MY SOUL

_____

_____

_____

FINANCIAL

_____

_____

_____

FROLICS

_____

_____

_____

End your day on a good note. List three things you are grateful for:

1. _____

2. _____

3. _____

Learn From Their Journey

🦋 Make It A Great Day

Three things you will accomplish today:

- ❑ _____
- ❑ _____
- ❑ _____

As you move through your day, pour into yourself. Then, make note of it:

FAITH

_____
_____
_____

FAMILY

_____
_____
_____

FITNESS

_____
_____
_____

You Can't Succeed If You Don't Try

FULL STEAM AHEAD

_____

_____

_____

FEED MY SOUL

_____

_____

_____

FINANCIAL

_____

_____

_____

FROLICS

_____

_____

_____

End your day on a good note. List three things you are grateful for:

1. _____

2. _____

3. _____

So Try

Notes

Good Morning

Three things you will accomplish today:

- ❏ _____
- ❏ _____
- ❏ _____

As you move through your day, pour into yourself. Then, make note of it:

FAITH

_____

_____

_____

FAMILY

_____

_____

_____

FITNESS

_____

_____

_____

If You Dream It, Believe In It

Date: _____

FULL STEAM AHEAD

_____

_____

_____

FEED MY SOUL

_____

_____

_____

FINANCIAL

_____

_____

_____

FROLICS

_____

_____

_____

End your day on a good note. List three things you are grateful for:

1. _____

2. _____

3. _____

Trust The Power Of Your Dreams

Three things you will accomplish today:

❑ ....

❑ ....

❑ ....

As you move through your day, pour into yourself. Then, make note of it:

FAITH

....

....

....

FAMILY

....

....

....

FITNESS

....

....

....

Expect A Lot

Date: _____

FULL STEAM AHEAD

_____

_____

_____

FEED MY SOUL

_____

_____

_____

FINANCIAL

_____

_____

_____

FROLICS

_____

_____

_____

End your day on a good note. List three things you are grateful for:

1. _____

2. _____

3. _____

Get A Lot

Rise & Grind

Three things you will accomplish today:

- ❏ _____
- ❏ _____
- ❏ _____

As you move through your day, pour into yourself. Then, make note of it:

FAITH

_____

_____

_____

FAMILY

_____

_____

_____

FITNESS

_____

_____

_____

Life Is Like A Boomerang

Date: _____

FULL STEAM AHEAD

_____

_____

_____

FEED MY SOUL

_____

_____

_____

FINANCIAL

_____

_____

_____

FROLICS

_____

_____

_____

End your day on a good note. List three things you are grateful for:

1. _____

2. _____

3. _____

What Are You Putting Out?

Time To Conquer The Day

Three things you will accomplish today:

❏ _____

❏ _____

❏ _____

As you move through your day, pour into yourself. Then, make note of it:

FAITH

_____

_____

_____

FAMILY

_____

_____

_____

FITNESS

_____

_____

_____

Energy Flows Where Attention Goes

Date: _____

FULL STEAM AHEAD

_____

_____

_____

FEED MY SOUL

_____

_____

_____

FINANCIAL

_____

_____

_____

FROLICS

_____

_____

_____

End your day on a good note. List three things you are grateful for:

1. _____

2. _____

3. _____

What Are You Focused On?

Out Of Bed, Sleepie Head

Three things you will accomplish today:

- ❏ _____
- ❏ _____
- ❏ _____

As you move through your day, pour into yourself. Then, make note of it:

FAITH

_____

_____

_____

FAMILY

_____

_____

_____

FITNESS

_____

_____

_____

Self-Development Is Essential

Date: _____

FULL STEAM AHEAD

_____

_____

_____

FEED MY SOUL

_____

_____

_____

FINANCIAL

_____

_____

_____

FROLICS

_____

_____

_____

End your day on a good note. List three things you are grateful for:

1. _____

2. _____

3. _____

Embrace What Allows You To Grow

Three things you will accomplish today:

❏ _____

❏ _____

❏ _____

As you move through your day, pour into yourself. Then, make note of it:

FAITH

_____

_____

_____

FAMILY

_____

_____

_____

FITNESS

_____

_____

_____

If It's All Important, Nothing's Important

Date: _____

FULL STEAM AHEAD

_____

_____

_____

FEED MY SOUL

_____

_____

_____

FINANCIAL

_____

_____

_____

FROLICS

_____

_____

_____

End your day on a good note. List three things you are grateful for:

1. _____

2. _____

3. _____

Prioritize

The Day Is Unfolding

Three things you will accomplish today:

❑ _____

❑ _____

❑ _____

As you move through your day, pour into yourself. Then, make note of it:

FAITH

_____

_____

_____

FAMILY

_____

_____

_____

FITNESS

_____

_____

_____

Life Is Short

Date: _____

FULL STEAM AHEAD

_____

_____

_____

FEED MY SOUL

_____

_____

_____

FINANCIAL

_____

_____

_____

FROLICS

_____

_____

_____

End your day on a good note. List three things you are grateful for:

1. _____

2. _____

3. _____

Eliminate What Does Not Bring You Joy

Notes

The Day Is Yours

Three things you will accomplish today:

- ☐ _____
- ☐ _____
- ☐ _____

As you move through your day, pour into yourself. Then, make note of it:

FAITH

_____

_____

_____

FAMILY

_____

_____

_____

FITNESS

_____

_____

_____

Who Are You?

Date: _____

FULL STEAM AHEAD

_____

_____

_____

FEED MY SOUL

_____

_____

_____

FINANCIAL

_____

_____

_____

FROLICS

_____

_____

_____

End your day on a good note. List three things you are grateful for:

1. _____

2. _____

3. _____

You Get To Decide

Welcome To A New Day

Three things you will accomplish today:

- ❏ _____
- ❏ _____
- ❏ _____

As you move through your day, pour into yourself. Then, make note of it:

FAITH

_____

_____

_____

FAMILY

_____

_____

_____

FITNESS

_____

_____

_____

What Do You Align Your Identity With?

Date: _____

FULL STEAM AHEAD

_____

_____

_____

FEED MY SOUL

_____

_____

_____

FINANCIAL

_____

_____

_____

FROLICS

_____

_____

_____

End your day on a good note. List three things you are grateful for:

1. _____

2. _____

3. _____

Be A Reflection Of What You Want To See

Hello There

Three things you will accomplish today:

❑ _____

❑ _____

❑ _____

As you move through your day, pour into yourself. Then, make note of it:

FAITH

_____

_____

_____

FAMILY

_____

_____

_____

FITNESS

_____

_____

_____

What Story Do You Need To Let Go Of?

FULL STEAM AHEAD

_____

_____

_____

FEED MY SOUL

_____

_____

_____

FINANCIAL

_____

_____

_____

FROLICS

_____

_____

_____

End your day on a good note. List three things you are grateful for:

1. _____

2. _____

3. _____

Release Yourself

Let's Do This

Three things you will accomplish today:

- [ ] _____
- [ ] _____
- [ ] _____

As you move through your day, pour into yourself. Then, make note of it:

FAITH

_____

_____

_____

FAMILY

_____

_____

_____

FITNESS

_____

_____

_____

There Is Beauty In Vulnerability

Date: _____

FULL STEAM AHEAD

_____

_____

_____

FEED MY SOUL

_____

_____

_____

FINANCIAL

_____

_____

_____

FROLICS

_____

_____

_____

End your day on a good note. List three things you are grateful for:

1. _____

2. _____

3. _____

Show Your True Self

Early Bird Catches The Worm

Three things you will accomplish today:

- ❏ _____
- ❏ _____
- ❏ _____

As you move through your day, pour into yourself. Then, make note of it:

FAITH

_____

_____

_____

FAMILY

_____

_____

_____

FITNESS

_____

_____

_____

Feel Every Emotion

Date: _____

FULL STEAM AHEAD

_____

_____

_____

FEED MY SOUL

_____

_____

_____

FINANCIAL

_____

_____

_____

FROLICS

_____

_____

_____

End your day on a good note. List three things you are grateful for:

1. _____

2. _____

3. _____

Accept. Process. Move On

Good Morning, Sunshine

Three things you will accomplish today:

❏ _____

❏ _____

❏ _____

As you move through your day, pour into yourself. Then, make note of it:

FAITH

_____

_____

_____

FAMILY

_____

_____

_____

FITNESS

_____

_____

_____

Let Go Of Limiting Beliefs

Date: _____

FULL STEAM AHEAD

_____

_____

_____

FEED MY SOUL

_____

_____

_____

FINANCIAL

_____

_____

_____

FROLICS

_____

_____

_____

End your day on a good note. List three things you are grateful for:

1. _____

2. _____

3. _____

You Are Capable Of Greatness

Make It A Great Day

Three things you will accomplish today:

❏ _____

❏ _____

❏ _____

As you move through your day, pour into yourself. Then, make note of it:

FAITH

_____

_____

_____

FAMILY

_____

_____

_____

FITNESS

_____

_____

_____

Relationships Are Two-Way Streets

Date: _____

FULL STEAM AHEAD

_____

_____

_____

FEED MY SOUL

_____

_____

_____

FINANCIAL

_____

_____

_____

FROLICS

_____

_____

_____

End your day on a good note. List three things you are grateful for:

1. _____

2. _____

3. _____

How Do You Show Up In Yours?

Notes

Good Morning

Three things you will accomplish today:

- ❑ _____
- ❑ _____
- ❑ _____

As you move through your day, pour into yourself. Then, make note of it:

FAITH

_____

_____

_____

FAMILY

_____

_____

_____

FITNESS

_____

_____

_____

Be Better Today Than You Were Yesterday

Date: _____

FULL STEAM AHEAD

_____

_____

_____

FEED MY SOUL

_____

_____

_____

FINANCIAL

_____

_____

_____

FROLICS

_____

_____

_____

End your day on a good note. List three things you are grateful for:

1. _____

2. _____

3. _____

You Only Need To Compete With Yourself

Upsie Daisie

Three things you will accomplish today:

❏ _____

❏ _____

❏ _____

As you move through your day, pour into yourself. Then, make note of it:

FAITH

_____

_____

_____

FAMILY

_____

_____

_____

FITNESS

_____

_____

_____

Embrace Change

Date: _____

FULL STEAM AHEAD

_____
_____
_____

FEED MY SOUL

_____
_____
_____

FINANCIAL

_____
_____
_____

FROLICS

_____
_____
_____

End your day on a good note. List three things you are grateful for:

1. _____
2. _____
3. _____

We Are Not Meant To Stay The Same

Rise & Grind

Three things you will accomplish today:

- ❑ _____
- ❑ _____
- ❑ _____

As you move through your day, pour into yourself. Then, make note of it:

FAITH

_____

_____

_____

FAMILY

_____

_____

_____

FITNESS

_____

_____

_____

The Compound Effect Is Real

Date: _____

FULL STEAM AHEAD

_____

_____

_____

FEED MY SOUL

_____

_____

_____

FINANCIAL

_____

_____

_____

FROLICS

_____

_____

_____

End your day on a good note. List three things you are grateful for:

1. _____

2. _____

3. _____

... and It Works Both Ways

Time To Conquer The Day

Three things you will accomplish today:

❏ _____

❏ _____

❏ _____

As you move through your day, pour into yourself. Then, make note of it:

FAITH

_____

_____

_____

FAMILY

_____

_____

_____

FITNESS

_____

_____

_____

Everything You Need Is Within

Date: _____

FULL STEAM AHEAD

_____

_____

_____

FEED MY SOUL

_____

_____

_____

FINANCIAL

_____

_____

_____

FROLICS

_____

_____

_____

End your day on a good note. List three things you are grateful for:

1. _____

2. _____

3. _____

Align The Pieces & Thrive

Out Of Bed, Sleepie Head

Three things you will accomplish today:

❑ _____

❑ _____

❑ _____

As you move through your day, pour into yourself. Then, make note of it:

FAITH

_____

_____

_____

FAMILY

_____

_____

_____

FITNESS

_____

_____

_____

Make A Schedule

Date: _____

FULL STEAM AHEAD

_____

_____

_____

FEED MY SOUL

_____

_____

_____

FINANCIAL

_____

_____

_____

FROLICS

_____

_____

_____

End your day on a good note. List three things you are grateful for:

1. _____

2. _____

3. _____

... and Stick To It

Early To Rise

Three things you will accomplish today:

❑ _____

❑ _____

❑ _____

As you move through your day, pour into yourself. Then, make note of it:

FAITH

_____

_____

_____

FAMILY

_____

_____

_____

FITNESS

_____

_____

_____

The Time May Never Be Perfect

Date: _____

FULL STEAM AHEAD

_____
_____
_____

FEED MY SOUL

_____
_____
_____

FINANCIAL

_____
_____
_____

FROLICS

_____
_____
_____

End your day on a good note. List three things you are grateful for:

1. _____
2. _____
3. _____

Just Start

The Day Is Unfolding

Three things you will accomplish today:

❑ _____

❑ _____

❑ _____

As you move through your day, pour into yourself. Then, make note of it:

FAITH

_____

_____

_____

FAMILY

_____

_____

_____

FITNESS

_____

_____

_____

What You Tell Yourself Matters

Date: _____

FULL STEAM AHEAD

_____

_____

_____

FEED MY SOUL

_____

_____

_____

FINANCIAL

_____

_____

_____

FROLICS

_____

_____

_____

End your day on a good note. List three things you are grateful for:

1. _____

2. _____

3. _____

Do You Need To Change The Narrative?

Notes

The Day Is Yours

Three things you will accomplish today:

❑ _____

❑ _____

❑ _____

As you move through your day, pour into yourself. Then, make note of it:

FAITH

_____

_____

_____

FAMILY

_____

_____

_____

FITNESS

_____

_____

_____

Dream Like A Child

Date: _____

FULL STEAM AHEAD

_____

_____

_____

FEED MY SOUL

_____

_____

_____

FINANCIAL

_____

_____

_____

FROLICS

_____

_____

_____

End your day on a good note. List three things you are grateful for:

1. _____

2. _____

3. _____

Let Your Imagination Run Free

Welcome To A New Day

Three things you will accomplish today:

❏ _____

❏ _____

❏ _____

As you move through your day, pour into yourself. Then, make note of it:

FAITH

_____

_____

_____

FAMILY

_____

_____

_____

FITNESS

_____

_____

_____

When You Look Good, You Feel Good

Date: _____

FULL STEAM AHEAD

_____

_____

_____

FEED MY SOUL

_____

_____

_____

FINANCIAL

_____

_____

_____

FROLICS

_____

_____

_____

End your day on a good note. List three things you are grateful for:

1. _____

2. _____

3. _____

Pamper Yourself

Hello There

Three things you will accomplish today:

☐ _____

☐ _____

☐ _____

As you move through your day, pour into yourself. Then, make note of it:

FAITH

_____

_____

_____

FAMILY

_____

_____

_____

FITNESS

_____

_____

_____

Dream It, Achieve It

FULL STEAM AHEAD

_____

_____

_____

FEED MY SOUL

_____

_____

_____

FINANCIAL

_____

_____

_____

FROLICS

_____

_____

_____

End your day on a good note. List three things you are grateful for:

1. _____

2. _____

3. _____

It CAN Happen

Let's Do This

Three things you will accomplish today:

- ❏ ....
- ❏ ....
- ❏ ....

As you move through your day, pour into yourself. Then, make note of it:

FAITH

....

....

....

FAMILY

....

....

....

FITNESS

....

....

....

Protect Your Peace

Date: _____

FULL STEAM AHEAD

_____

_____

_____

FEED MY SOUL

_____

_____

_____

FINANCIAL

_____

_____

_____

FROLICS

_____

_____

_____

End your day on a good note. List three things you are grateful for:

1. _____

2. _____

3. _____

... At All Costs

Early Bird Catches The Worm

Three things you will accomplish today:

❏ _____

❏ _____

❏ _____

As you move through your day, pour into yourself. Then, make note of it:

FAITH

_____

_____

_____

FAMILY

_____

_____

_____

FITNESS

_____

_____

_____

Hope Is A Treasure

FULL STEAM AHEAD

_____

_____

_____

FEED MY SOUL

_____

_____

_____

FINANCIAL

_____

_____

_____

FROLICS

_____

_____

_____

End your day on a good note. List three things you are grateful for:

1. _____

2. _____

3. _____

Don't Lose It

Good Morning, Sunshine

Three things you will accomplish today:

☐ _____

☐ _____

☐ _____

As you move through your day, pour into yourself. Then, make note of it:

FAITH

_____

_____

_____

FAMILY

_____

_____

_____

FITNESS

_____

_____

_____

Look Forward

Date: _____

FULL STEAM AHEAD

_____

_____

_____

FEED MY SOUL

_____

_____

_____

FINANCIAL

_____

_____

_____

FROLICS

_____

_____

_____

End your day on a good note. List three things you are grateful for:

1. _____

2. _____

3. _____

Your Best Days Are Ahead

Make It A Great Day

Three things you will accomplish today:

❑ _____

❑ _____

❑ _____

As you move through your day, pour into yourself. Then, make note of it:

FAITH

_____

_____

_____

FAMILY

_____

_____

_____

FITNESS

_____

_____

_____

Therapy Is For The Strong

Date: _____

FULL STEAM AHEAD

_____

_____

_____

FEED MY SOUL

_____

_____

_____

FINANCIAL

_____

_____

_____

FROLICS

_____

_____

_____

End your day on a good note. List three things you are grateful for:

1. _____

2. _____

3. _____

Mental Health Is The Key To Health

Notes

Good Morning

Three things you will accomplish today:

- ❑ _____
- ❑ _____
- ❑ _____

As you move through your day, pour into yourself. Then, make note of it:

FAITH

_____

_____

_____

FAMILY

_____

_____

_____

FITNESS

_____

_____

_____

Mindset Is Everything

Date: _____

FULL STEAM AHEAD

_____

_____

_____

FEED MY SOUL

_____

_____

_____

FINANCIAL

_____

_____

_____

FROLICS

_____

_____

_____

End your day on a good note. List three things you are grateful for:

1. _____

2. _____

3. _____

Positive Vibes Only

Upsie Daisie

Three things you will accomplish today:

❑ _____

❑ _____

❑ _____

As you move through your day, pour into yourself. Then, make note of it:

FAITH

_____

_____

_____

FAMILY

_____

_____

_____

FITNESS

_____

_____

_____

Change Your Scenery

Date: _____

FULL STEAM AHEAD

_____

_____

_____

FEED MY SOUL

_____

_____

_____

FINANCIAL

_____

_____

_____

FROLICS

_____

_____

_____

End your day on a good note. List three things you are grateful for:

1. _____

2. _____

3. _____

Explore Some Place New Today

Rise & Grind

Three things you will accomplish today:

- ☐ _____
- ☐ _____
- ☐ _____

As you move through your day, pour into yourself. Then, make note of it:

FAITH

_____

_____

_____

FAMILY

_____

_____

_____

FITNESS

_____

_____

_____

Music Soothes The Soul

Date: _____

FULL STEAM AHEAD

_____

_____

_____

FEED MY SOUL

_____

_____

_____

FINANCIAL

_____

_____

_____

FROLICS

_____

_____

_____

End your day on a good note. List three things you are grateful for:

1. _____

2. _____

3. _____

Play Your Favorite Song

Time To Conquer The Day

Three things you will accomplish today:

- ❑ _____
- ❑ _____
- ❑ _____

As you move through your day, pour into yourself. Then, make note of it:

FAITH

_____

_____

_____

FAMILY

_____

_____

_____

FITNESS

_____

_____

_____

Laughter Lifts Your Spirits

Date: _____

FULL STEAM AHEAD

_____

_____

_____

FEED MY SOUL

_____

_____

_____

FINANCIAL

_____

_____

_____

FROLICS

_____

_____

_____

End your day on a good note. List three things you are grateful for:

1. _____

2. _____

3. _____

Watch Your Favorite Comedy

Out Of Bed, Sleepie Head

Three things you will accomplish today:

❏ _____

❏ _____

❏ _____

As you move through your day, pour into yourself. Then, make note of it:

FAITH

_____

_____

_____

FAMILY

_____

_____

_____

FITNESS

_____

_____

_____

Spread Kindness

Date: _____

FULL STEAM AHEAD

_____

_____

_____

FEED MY SOUL

_____

_____

_____

FINANCIAL

_____

_____

_____

FROLICS

_____

_____

_____

End your day on a good note. List three things you are grateful for:

1. _____

2. _____

3. _____

Share A Smile With Someone

Three things you will accomplish today:

❑ _____

❑ _____

❑ _____

As you move through your day, pour into yourself. Then, make note of it:

FAITH

_____

_____

_____

FAMILY

_____

_____

_____

FITNESS

_____

_____

_____

Put Down The Camera

Date: _____

FULL STEAM AHEAD

_____

_____

_____

FEED MY SOUL

_____

_____

_____

FINANCIAL

_____

_____

_____

FROLICS

_____

_____

_____

End your day on a good note. List three things you are grateful for:

1. _____

2. _____

3. _____

Actually Live In & Enjoy The Moment

The Day Is Unfolding

Three things you will accomplish today:

- ❑ _____
- ❑ _____
- ❑ _____

As you move through your day, pour into yourself. Then, make note of it:

FAITH

_____

_____

_____

FAMILY

_____

_____

_____

FITNESS

_____

_____

_____

Go On An Electronics Fast

Date: _____

FULL STEAM AHEAD

_____

_____

_____

FEED MY SOUL

_____

_____

_____

FINANCIAL

_____

_____

_____

FROLICS

_____

_____

_____

End your day on a good note. List three things you are grateful for:

1. _____

2. _____

3. _____

24 Hours ... No Distractions

Notes

Welcome To A New Day

Three things you will accomplish today:

❏ _____

❏ _____

❏ _____

As you move through your day, pour into yourself. Then, make note of it:

FAITH

_____

_____

_____

FAMILY

_____

_____

_____

FITNESS

_____

_____

_____

Define Success For Yourself

Date: _____

FULL STEAM AHEAD

_____

_____

_____

FEED MY SOUL

_____

_____

_____

FINANCIAL

_____

_____

_____

FROLICS

_____

_____

_____

End your day on a good note. List three things you are grateful for:

1. _____

2. _____

3. _____

Carve Your Own Path

The Day Is Yours

Three things you will accomplish today:

❑ _____

❑ _____

❑ _____

As you move through your day, pour into yourself. Then, make note of it:

FAITH

_____

_____

_____

FAMILY

_____

_____

_____

FITNESS

_____

_____

_____

What Do You Desire?

Date: _____

FULL STEAM AHEAD

_____

_____

_____

FEED MY SOUL

_____

_____

_____

FINANCIAL

_____

_____

_____

FROLICS

_____

_____

_____

End your day on a good note. List three things you are grateful for:

1. _____

2. _____

3. _____

Reach Out & Touch Your Dreams

Hello There

Three things you will accomplish today:

- ❏ _____
- ❏ _____
- ❏ _____

As you move through your day, pour into yourself. Then, make note of it:

FAITH

_____

_____

_____

FAMILY

_____

_____

_____

FITNESS

_____

_____

_____

Celebrate Your Wins

FULL STEAM AHEAD

_____

_____

_____

FEED MY SOUL

_____

_____

_____

FINANCIAL

_____

_____

_____

FROLICS

_____

_____

_____

End your day on a good note. List three things you are grateful for:

1. _____

2. _____

3. _____

You Accomplish More Than You Realize

Let's Do This

Three things you will accomplish today:

❏ _____

❏ _____

❏ _____

As you move through your day, pour into yourself. Then, make note of it:

FAITH

_____

_____

_____

FAMILY

_____

_____

_____

FITNESS

_____

_____

_____

It's OK To End Toxic Relationships

Date: _____

FULL STEAM AHEAD

_____

_____

_____

FEED MY SOUL

_____

_____

_____

FINANCIAL

_____

_____

_____

FROLICS

_____

_____

_____

End your day on a good note. List three things you are grateful for:

1. _____

2. _____

3. _____

Embrace Your Tribe; Ignore The Rest

Make It A Great Day

Three things you will accomplish today:

❑ _____

❑ _____

❑ _____

As you move through your day, pour into yourself. Then, make note of it:

FAITH

_____

_____

_____

FAMILY

_____

_____

_____

FITNESS

_____

_____

_____

You Don't Need All The Answers

Date: _____

FULL STEAM AHEAD

_____

_____

_____

FEED MY SOUL

_____

_____

_____

FINANCIAL

_____

_____

_____

FROLICS

_____

_____

_____

End your day on a good note. List three things you are grateful for:

1. _____

2. _____

3. _____

Start Where You Are

Good Morning, Sunshine

Three things you will accomplish today:

❑ _____

❑ _____

❑ _____

As you move through your day, pour into yourself. Then, make note of it:

FAITH

_____

_____

_____

FAMILY

_____

_____

_____

FITNESS

_____

_____

_____

Define Your Values

Date: _____

FULL STEAM AHEAD

_____

_____

_____

FEED MY SOUL

_____

_____

_____

FINANCIAL

_____

_____

_____

FROLICS

_____

_____

_____

End your day on a good note. List three things you are grateful for:

1. _____

2. _____

3. _____

Then Align Your Actions With Them

Make It A Great Day

Three things you will accomplish today:

❑ _____

❑ _____

❑ _____

As you move through your day, pour into yourself. Then, make note of it:

FAITH

_____

_____

_____

FAMILY

_____

_____

_____

FITNESS

_____

_____

_____

Relax

FULL STEAM AHEAD

_____

_____

_____

FEED MY SOUL

_____

_____

_____

FINANCIAL

_____

_____

_____

FROLICS

_____

_____

_____

End your day on a good note. List three things you are grateful for:

1. _____

2. _____

3. _____

Recharge Your Batteries

Notes

Time To Order Another Journal ...

The Day Is Yours

Three things you will accomplish today:

- ❏ _____
- ❏ _____
- ❏ _____

As you move through your day, pour into yourself. Then, make note of it:

FAITH

_____
_____
_____

FAMILY

_____
_____
_____

FITNESS

_____
_____
_____

Dwelling On What Ifs Won't Change What Is

Date: _____

FULL STEAM AHEAD

_____

_____

_____

FEED MY SOUL

_____

_____

_____

FINANCIAL

_____

_____

_____

FROLICS

_____

_____

_____

End your day on a good note. List three things you are grateful for:

1. _____

2. _____

3. _____

Focus On NOW

Early Bird Catches The Worm

Three things you will accomplish today:

❑ _____

❑ _____

❑ _____

As you move through your day, pour into yourself. Then, make note of it:

FAITH

_____

_____

_____

FAMILY

_____

_____

_____

FITNESS

_____

_____

_____

Never Give Up

Date: _____

FULL STEAM AHEAD

_____

_____

_____

FEED MY SOUL

_____

_____

_____

FINANCIAL

_____

_____

_____

FROLICS

_____

_____

_____

End your day on a good note. List three things you are grateful for:

1. _____

2. _____

3. _____

Try Everything

Welcome To A New Day

Three things you will accomplish today:

- ❏ _____
- ❏ _____
- ❏ _____

As you move through your day, pour into yourself. Then, make note of it:

FAITH

_____

_____

_____

FAMILY

_____

_____

_____

FITNESS

_____

_____

_____

It's Not Just OK To Have Boundaries

Date: _____

FULL STEAM AHEAD

_____

_____

_____

FEED MY SOUL

_____

_____

_____

FINANCIAL

_____

_____

_____

FROLICS

_____

_____

_____

End your day on a good note. List three things you are grateful for:

1. _____

2. _____

3. _____

... It's Necessary

Let's Do This

Three things you will accomplish today:

❑ _____

❑ _____

❑ _____

As you move through your day, pour into yourself. Then, make note of it:

FAITH

_____

_____

_____

FAMILY

_____

_____

_____

FITNESS

_____

_____

_____

Leave The Past In The Past

Date: _____

FULL STEAM AHEAD

_____

_____

_____

FEED MY SOUL

_____

_____

_____

FINANCIAL

_____

_____

_____

FROLICS

_____

_____

_____

End your day on a good note. List three things you are grateful for:

1. _____

2. _____

3. _____

Carry Life Lessons Into The Future

Good Morning, Sunshine

Three things you will accomplish today:

☐ _____

☐ _____

☐ _____

As you move through your day, pour into yourself. Then, make note of it:

FAITH

_____

_____

_____

FAMILY

_____

_____

_____

FITNESS

_____

_____

_____

Give Yourself Grace

Date: _____

FULL STEAM AHEAD

_____

_____

_____

FEED MY SOUL

_____

_____

_____

FINANCIAL

_____

_____

_____

FROLICS

_____

_____

_____

End your day on a good note. List three things you are grateful for:

1. _____

2. _____

3. _____

It's Ok To Be A Work In Progress

Early Bird Catches The Worm

Three things you will accomplish today:

- ❏ _____
- ❏ _____
- ❏ _____

As you move through your day, pour into yourself. Then, make note of it:

FAITH

_____

_____

_____

FAMILY

_____

_____

_____

FITNESS

_____

_____

_____

Let It Go

Date: _____

FULL STEAM AHEAD

_____

_____

_____

FEED MY SOUL

_____

_____

_____

FINANCIAL

_____

_____

_____

FROLICS

_____

_____

_____

End your day on a good note. List three things you are grateful for:

1. _____

2. _____

3. _____

It Will Work Out In The End

🦋 90 Day Check-In

Consider what worked, what didn't work,
and what you may want to tweak for next quarter.

Notes

Notes

Notes

🦋 You Did It!

Congratulations! You made it through the entire 90 days. Pat yourself on the back. At this point you should feel accomplished and see progress on your goals. Your vision is even closer to becoming a reality and I am so very excited for you.

Now - continue to build on what you have accomplished. If you have not done so already .. order another journal so you can keep the progress going.

Want to see how far you've come? Keep this journal in a safe place and look back on it a year from now. You will be amazed at how much growth you experience when you are consistent, intentional, and gracious.

Thank you for trusting that my journal will help you move forward towards your vision. Know that as you walk your journey, I am walking alongside you and cheering you on every step of the way.

Now, let's keep growing together.

🦋 Author Bio

Nadia Gilkes is an Attorney, REALTOR®, and Author. Her first novel, *Woke Up Dead*, was published in 2019 and became a #1 Bestseller. *Woke Up Dead* can be found on Amazon and Barnes & Noble.

Ms. Gilkes is passionate about helping others preserve their legacies. By assisting clients with real estate transactions and estate planning, she is able to help others provide security for their families for generations to come.

Ms. Gilkes splits her time between the Dallas/Fort Worth Metroplex and Las Vegas, NV. In her spare time she enjoys quilting, rooting for her beloved Buffalo Bills, and watching P!nk videos on YouTube (while patiently awaiting her return to the concert stage).

Made in the USA
Las Vegas, NV
21 December 2021